PIANO • VOCAL • GUITAR

BLUE

CONTENTS

2 After The Love Has Gone
12 Among My Souvenirs
14 Are You Lonesome Tonight?
7 Black Coffee
16 Blossom Fell, A
19 Body And Soul
24 By Myself
28 By The Time I Get To Phoenix
30 Cottage For Sale, A
34 Crazy
36 Cry
38 Cry Me A River
40 Cryin' Time
42 Diary
46 Dinner For One, Please James
48 Don't Cry Out Loud
51 End Of A Love Affair, The
58 Feelings (¿Dime?)
64 For The Good Times
61 Have You Ever Been Lonely?
    (Have You Ever Been Blue?)
66 Here's That Rainy Day
74 How Am I Supposed To Live Without You
69 How Can We Be Lovers
80 How Insensitive (Insensatez)
84 I Apologize
88 I Can Dream, Can't I?
92 I Miss You So

95 I Will Wait For You
98 I Wish I Didn't Love You So
104 I Wish You Love
101 I'll Never Smile Again
108 I'm Sorry
110 It Only Hurts For A Little While
115 It Was Almost Like A Song
118 It's A Blue World
120 It's Easy To Remember
123 It's Too Late
126 Just One More Chance
134 Little Girl Blue
131 Love Is Blue (L'amour Est Bleu)
138 Love Letters In The Sand
140 Love On The Rocks
148 Neither One Of Us
    (Wants To Be The First To Say Goodbye)
154 So Far Away
158 Somebody Else Is Taking My Place
160 Sorry Seems To Be The Hardest Word
145 Stormy Weather
    (Keeps Rainin' All The Time)
164 Tell Me On A Sunday
168 Way We Were, The
171 What Now My Love
174 What's Forever For
177 Yesterday
180 You Don't Bring Me Flowers

This publication is not for sale in
the E.C. and/or Australia
or New Zealand.

ISBN 0-7935-3623-5

HAL•LEONARD
CORPORATION
7777 W. BLUEMOUND RD. P.O. BOX 13819 MILWAUKEE, WI 53213

AFTER THE LOVE HAS GONE

Words and Music by DAVID FOSTER,
JAY GRAYDON, and BILL CHAMPLIN

MCA music publishing

BLACK COFFEE

Words and Music by PAUL FRANCIS WEBSTER
and SONNY BURKE

Girl version: I'm

feel - in' might - y lone - some, have - n't slept a wink, I
feel - in' might - y lone - some, have - n't slept a wink, I

walk the floor and watch the door and in be - tween I drink black
walk the floor and watch the door and in be - tween I drink black

cof - fee. _____
cof - fee. _____

Love's a hand - me - down
Since my gal went a -

AMONG MY SOUVENIRS

Words by EDGAR LESLIE
Music by HORATIO NICHOLLS

ARE YOU LONESOME TONIGHT?

Words and Music by ROY TURK
and LOU HANDMAN

A BLOSSOM FELL

Words and Music by HOWARD BARNES,
HAROLD CORNELIUS and DOMINIC JOHN

BODY AND SOUL

Words by EDWARD HEYMAN,
ROBERT SOUR and FRANK EYTON
Music by JOHN GREEN

BY MYSELF
(From "BETWEEN THE DEVIL")

Words by HOWARD DIETZ
Music by ARTHUR SCHWARTZ

BY THE TIME I GET TO PHOENIX

Words and Music by
JIMMY WEBB

A COTTAGE FOR SALE

Words by LARRY CONLEY
Music by WILLARD ROBISON

empty and still,— Needing your love— to com - mand it.
sad-ness I feel,— What is this new— hope in - side me.

CHORUS

Our lit - tle dream cas - tle with ev - 'ry dream gone,— Is

lone-ly and si - lent, The shades are all drawn, And my heart is heav - y as

I gaze up - on— A Cot-tage For Sale——— The

face,   But when I   reach a   window,   There's emp - ty

space._____ The key's in the mail_ box the   same as be - fore,_   But

no one is wait - ing   for me an - y more,   The end of our sto - ry   is

told on the door_   A Cot-tage For Sale._____ Our Sale.

CRAZY

Words and Music by
WILLIE NELSON

CRY

Words and Music by
CHURCHILL KOHLMAN

CRY ME A RIVER

Words and Music by
ARTHUR HAMILTON

CRYIN' TIME

Words and Music by
BUCK OWENS

Now they say that ab-sence makes the heart grow fon-der,___ And that tears are on-ly rain to make love grow Well, my love for you could nev-er grow no strong-er,___ If I lived to be a hund-red years old. Oh, it's cry-in' time a-gain, you're gon-na leave me,___ I can see that far a-way look ___ in your

DIARY

Words and Music by
DAVID GATES

DINNER FOR ONE, PLEASE JAMES

Words and Music by
MICHAEL CARR

DON'T CRY OUT LOUD

Words and Music by CAROLE BAYER SAGER
and PETER ALLEN

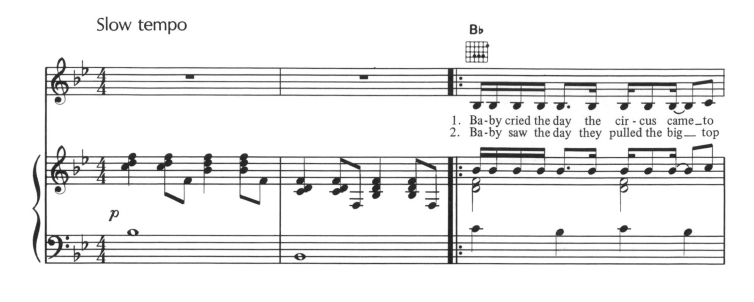

THE END OF A LOVE AFFAIR

Words and Music by
EDWARD C. REDDING

MCA music publishing

52

FEELINGS
(¿DIME?)

English Words and Music by MORRIS ALBERT
Spanish Lyric by THOMAS FUNDORA

HAVE YOU EVER BEEN LONELY?
(HAVE YOU EVER BEEN BLUE?)

Words by GEORGE BROWN
Music by PETER DeROSE

FOR THE GOOD TIMES

Words and Music by
KRIS KRISTOFFERSON

HERE'S THAT RAINY DAY

Words by JOHNNY BURKE
Music by JIMMY VAN HEUSEN

Very slow

Lyrics:

May-be I should have saved those left o-ver dreams; fun-ny, but here's that rain-y day. Here's that rain-y day they

HOW CAN WE BE LOVERS

Words and Music by DESMOND CHILD,
MICHAEL BOLTON and DIANE WARREN

Ba - by. _____ How can we be lov - ers? _____

HOW AM I SUPPOSED TO LIVE WITHOUT YOU

Words and Music by MICHAEL BOLTON
and DOUG JAMES

HOW INSENSITIVE
(INSENSATEZ)

Original Words by VINICIUS de MORAES
English Words by NORMAN GIMBEL
Music by ANTONIO CARLOS JOBIM

Moderately

How _____ in-sen-si-tive _____
Now, _____ {he's / she's} gone _ a - way _____

_ I must _ have seemed _____ when he told me that _ {he / she} loved _ me. _____
_ and I'm _ a - lone _____ with the mem-'ry of _ {his / her} last _ look. _____

Portuguese Lyrics

A insensatez
Que você fez
Coração mais sem cuidado
Fez chorar de dôr
O seu amôr
Um amôr tão delicado
Ah! Porque você
Foi fraco assim
Assim tão desalmado
Ah! Meu coração
Que nunca amou
Não merece ser amado
Vai meu coração
Ouve a razão
Usa só sinceridade
Quem semeia vento
Diz a razão
Colhe tempestade
Vai meu coração
Pede perdão
Perdão apaixonado
Vai porque
Quem não
Pede perdão
Não é nunca perdoado.

I APOLOGIZE

Words and Music by AL HOFFMAN,
AL GOODHART and ED NELSON

I'm sor-ry, so sor-ry. What more can I say?
I loved you, I lost you. Oh, what I've gone through!

Nev-er knew how much you meant to me till I went a-
Ev-er since the day I let you go I've been, oh, so

way. It's my fault, all my fault
blue! I loved you, I still do.

I CAN DREAM, CAN'T I?

Lyric by IRVING KAHAL
Music by SAMMY FAIN

I MISS YOU SO

Words and Music by JIMMY HENDERSON,
BERTHA SCOTT and SID ROBIN

I WILL WAIT FOR YOU

(From "THE UMBRELLAS OF CHERBOURG")

Music by MICHEL LEGRAND
Original French Text by JACQUES DEMY
English Lyrics by NORMAN GIMBEL

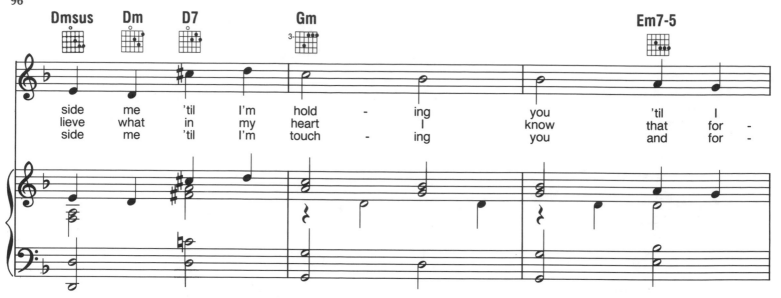

side me 'til I'm hold - ing you 'til I
lieve what in my heart I know that for -
side me 'til I'm touch - ing you and for -

hear you sigh here in my arms. An - y
ev - er more I'll wait for
ev - er more shar - ing your

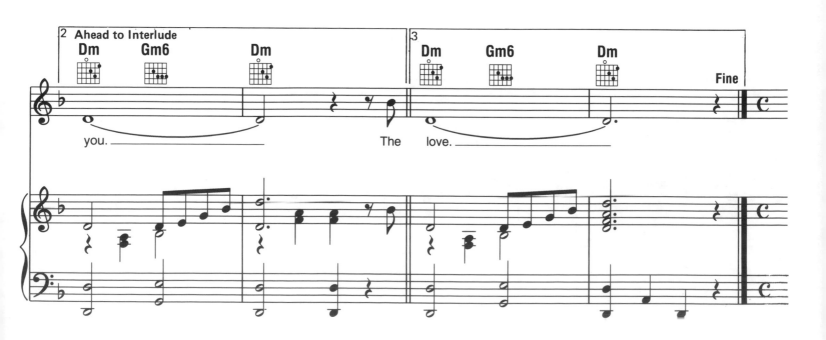

you. _____ The love.

I WISH I DIDN'T LOVE YOU SO

(From The Paramount Picture "THE PERILS OF PAULINE")

Words and Music by
FRANK LOESSER

I'LL NEVER SMILE AGAIN

Words and Music by
RUTH LOWE

I WISH YOU LOVE

English Lyric by ALBERT A. BEACH
French Lyric and Music by CHARLES TRENET

I'M SORRY

Words and Music by RONNIE SELF
and DUB ALBRITTEN

IT ONLY HURTS FOR A LITTLE WHILE

Words and Music by MACK DAVID
and FRED SPIELMAN

IT WAS ALMOST LIKE A SONG

Lyric by HAL DAVID
Music by ARCHIE JORDAN

Once in ev-'ry life,   some-one comes a-
You were in my arms,   just where you be-

long,   and you came to me.
long,   we were so in love.

IT'S A BLUE WORLD

Words and Music by BOB WRIGHT
and CHET FORREST

IT'S EASY TO REMEMBER
(From The Paramount Picture "MISSISSIPPI")

Words by LORENZ HART
Music by RICHARD RODGERS

IT'S TOO LATE

Words by TONI STERN
Music by CAROLE KING

JUST ONE MORE CHANCE

Words by SAM COSLOW
Music by ARTHUR JOHNSTON

Just one more chance, __ to prove it's you a - lone I

care for, each night I say a lit - tle

pray'r for just one more chance. __

Just one more night, __ to taste the kiss - es that en -

LOVE IS BLUE
(L'AMOUR EST BLEU)

English Lyric by BRIAN BLACKBURN
Original French Lyric by PIERRE COUR
Music by ANDRE POPP

LITTLE GIRL BLUE

Words by LORENZ HART
Music by RICHARD RODGERS

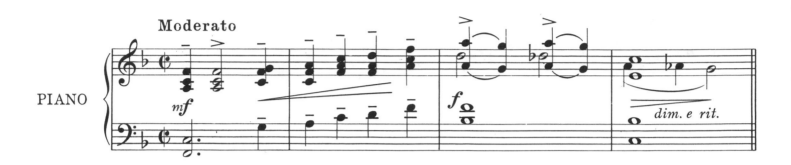

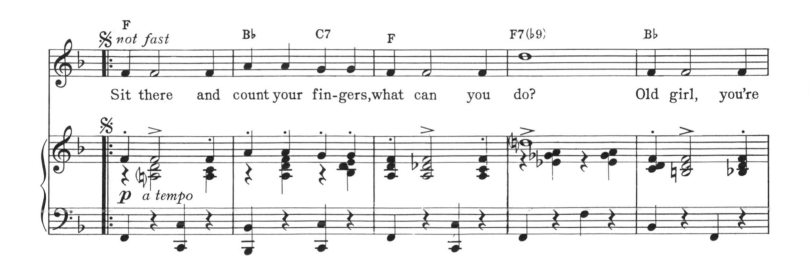

Sit there and count your fin-gers, what can you do? Old girl, you're

through. Sit there and count your lit-tle fin-gers, Un-

LOVE LETTERS IN THE SAND

Words by NICK KENNY and CHARLES KENNY
Music by J. FRED COOTS

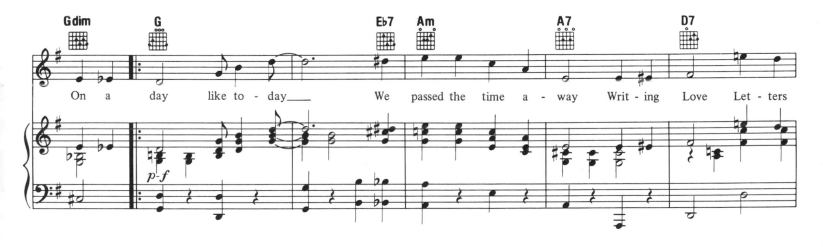

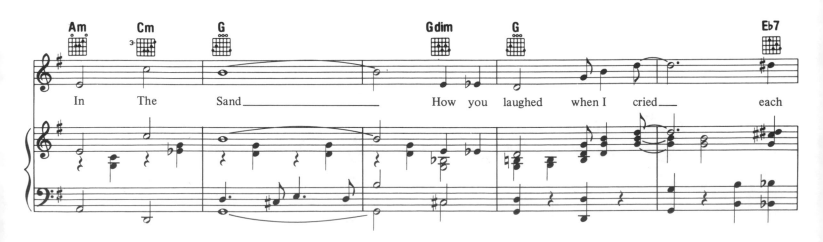

LOVE ON THE ROCKS

(From The Motion Picture "THE JAZZ SINGER")

Words and Music by NEIL DIAMOND
and GILBERT BECAUD

STORMY WEATHER
(KEEPS RAININ' ALL THE TIME)

Lyrics by TED KOEHLER
Music by HAROLD ARLEN

Slow lament

NEITHER ONE OF US
(WANTS TO BE THE FIRST TO SAY GOODBYE)

Words and Music by
JIM WEATHERLY

SO FAR AWAY

Words and Music by
CAROLE KING

SOMEBODY ELSE IS TAKING MY PLACE

Words and Music by DICK HOWARD,
BOB ELLSWORTH and RUSS MORGAN

SORRY SEEMS TO BE THE HARDEST WORD

Words and Music by ELTON JOHN
and BERNIE TAUPIN

TELL ME ON A SUNDAY
(From "SONG & DANCE")

Music by ANDREW LLOYD WEBBER
Lyrics by DON BLACK

Don't write a let-ter
when you want to leave.
Don't call me at three A. M.
from a friend's a-part-ment, I'd like to choose how I

Let me down ea-sy,
no big song and dance.
No long fa-ces, no long looks,
no deep con-ver-sa-tion, I know the way we should

THE WAY WE WERE

Words by ALAN and MARILYN BERGMAN
Music by MARVIN HAMLISCH

Mem - 'ries _____ light the cor - ners of my mind.
pic - tures _____ of the smiles we left be - hind,
Mem - 'ries _____ may be beau - ti - ful, and yet,

Mist - y wa - ter col - or mem - 'ries _____ of the way we
smiles we gave to one an - oth - er _____ for the way we
what's too pain - ful to re - mem - ber _____

WHAT NOW MY LOVE
(Original French Title: "ET MAINTENANT")

Original French Lyric by PIERRE DELANOE
Music by GILBERT BECAUD
English Adaptation by CARL SIGMAN

Moderate Bolero tempo

WHAT'S FOREVER FOR

Words and Music by
RAFE VanHOY

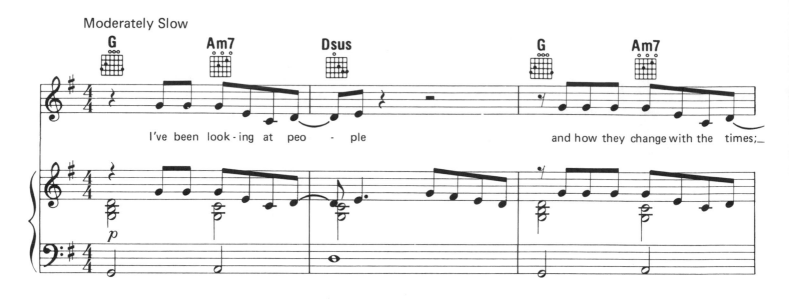

I've been look-ing at peo - ple and how they change with the times;

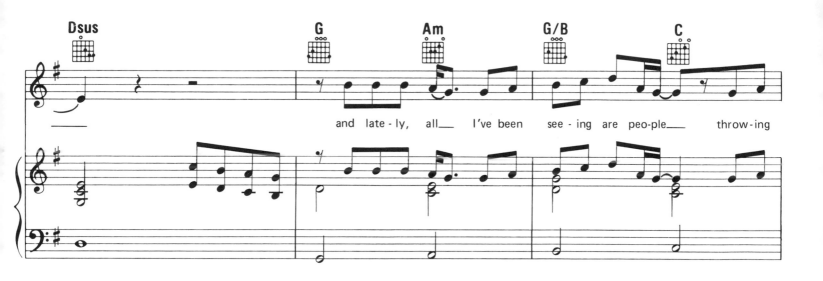

and late-ly, all__ I've been see-ing are peo-ple__ throw-ing

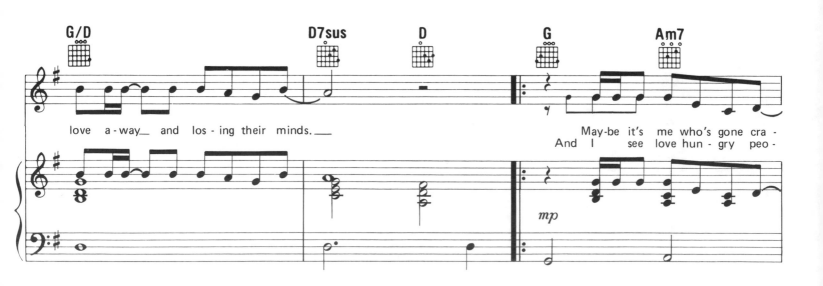

love a-way__ and los-ing their minds.__

May-be it's me who's gone cra-
And I see love hun-gry peo-

an-y-bod-y ev-er stay____ to - geth - er an-y-more?____

And if love____ nev-er lasts for - ev-er, tell me: What's for - ev - er for?__

To Coda ⊕

D.S. al Coda

CODA ⊕

decresc.

rit.

YESTERDAY

Words and Music by JOHN LENNON
and PAUL McCARTNEY

YOU DON'T BRING ME FLOWERS

Words by NEIL DIAMOND,
MARILYN BERGMAN and ALAN BERGMAN
Music by NEIL DIAMOND

Slowly and freely

You don't bring me flow-ers; you don't sing me love songs.

You hard-ly talk to me an-y-more when you come through the door at the end of the day.

I re-mem-ber when you could-n't wait to love me,